A GUIDE TO HELP

CLUB
ADVISORS
THRIVE

TAWAN PERRY

COPYRIGHT NOTICE

PUBLISHER'S NOTE

Due to the dynamic nature of the Internet, any web addresses or links contained in this book may have changed since publication and may no longer be valid. This publication is designed to provide accurate and authoritative information in regard to the subject matter covered. It is sold with the understanding that the author and publisher are not engaged in rendering legal, accounting or other professional services. If you require legal advice or other expert assistance, you should seek the services of a competent professional.

TABLE OF CONTENTS

3

ACKNOWLEDGMENTS

Cynthia * You are truly a blessing. Your work is incredible, and I'm so glad you're on my team.

Ayman * Your artistry is a gift from above. Thanks for everything.

Wendy * Thanks for inspiring me to write this book.

Carlos * Thanks for all of your advice, ideas, and for being such a great friend over the years.

All My Organization Advisors * Thanks for all the hard work that you put in. Never forget that you make a difference in more lives than you will ever imagine.

TO ALL STUDENT ORGANIZATION ADVISORS

As a former student organization advisor, I completely understand the daily challenges that organization advisors encounter. I've written this book with you in mind. This guide covers several important topics, such as getting faculty buy-in, assessing events, and writing learning outcomes for your events. Whether you are a first-time advisor or a seasoned advisor, this guide will help you to better serve student leaders and create an enriching campus environment.

Organization advisors will also discover:

- How to effortlessly transition student leaders from one year to the next
- Creative ways to motivate unenthusiastic student leaders
- How to masterfully balance home and work life
- How to market events that will result in standing room only attendance

- How to organize a well-attended conference from start to finish
- Resourceful ideas that will help you uphold your budget
- Fun and affordable programming ideas, sample event calendars, and assessment forms

This innovative book is perfect for:

☑ Student Activity Directors/Coordinators
☑ Greek Advisors
☑ Club and Student Organization Advisors
☑ First Year Experience Directors
☑ Residence Life Professionals
☑ Graduate Assistants

Thank you for your investment in this book and your trust in my expertise to help you in your professional career.

Tawan Perry, M.Ed.

INTRODUCTION

It's not easy being in your position. Most higher education professionals have meetings to attend, events to plan, and general planning, and sometimes the job itself can be overwhelming, daunting, and time-consuming. I wrote this book as a guide that would be easy to follow and continue to influence and empower leaders.

This guide is meant for student organization advisors and directors who are working with students on a day-to-day basis, helping to build student leadership organizations.

Whether you are doing this for the very first time or you are a seasoned advisor, this book is for you. It is written to give you practical advice that you can readily use to help you begin to build your organizations, as well as avoid some of the common mistakes of many advisors.

Reading this book and using all of the materials provided will quickly give you the results you're looking for with your organization. It is intended to help you improve your skills as an advisor, so that you may be a better asset to your student leaders, who, in turn, will be better assets to your campus.

Tawan Perry, M.Ed.

CHAPTER 1

Keeping Your Budget

"When you get to the end of your rope, tie a knot and hang on." Franklin D. Roosevelt

These days, it seems that everyone is dealing with budget cuts. Whether you're a small school, a big school, a private school or a community college, every school has been dealing with fiscal adjustments within their institutions. Now more than ever, it's all about using your funds appropriately, getting the best deal, and being able to justify how and why you're using this money.

Gone are the days when you can just spend money however you want to without a need for explanations. Gone are the days where you can spend money and not have it accounted for, penny for penny. In this, chapter I discuss ways to not only account for your budget, but also how to stretch your budget and make it work harder for you and your students.

Tip #1: Find out where you are.

In order to decide how much money you can spend for your school year or semester, it's a great idea to know exactly how much money you have. The best way to find that out is by talking to the appropriate resources who endow you with your budget.

Once you have a solid foundation, or once you figure out where you are with your budget, you then have an opportunity to begin figuring out how to best allocate your budget to which programs, activities, and other expenses you may have.

Tip #2: Decide where your big dollars will go first.

One rule of thumb for any budget is to decide where you want to spend your money first. The best way to determine this is to decide what events on your campus have been significant and where money for these must be spent.

For example, if you always plan a conference in the spring, it's best to decide how much money you will need for that right at the start before you begin allocating for other events. As we all know, when you're spending money, it can quickly walk away. So your first objective is to figure out where your big dollars will go first.

Tip #3: Set aside discretionary funds.

The purpose of setting aside discretionary funds is quite simply because things happen, and you want to make sure that you will be covered for all of the challenges you may face throughout the year. Setting aside discretionary funds more or less serves as a back-up plan, and when it's necessary to use them, make sure that you use them for some of the smaller things you may have to spend money on later in the year.

This is a great strategy to help you stretch your budget, so that you're never in a situation where you find yourself trying to overspend at the end of the year.

Tip #4: Put a system in place to organize your spending.

When you put a funding system in place, make sure that all of your spending is accounted for. This is an important bookkeeping practice that you want to develop and get in the habit of developing and sticking to.

You want to use spreadsheets and physical files with receipts. Hold on to all of your credit card statements and keep everything in order, so that at the end of the year or the semester, or whenever you are expected to give a full account of your expense report, you are completely organized.

I know it seems like a no-brainer, but for many people this is something they don't really practice. However, it is absolutely one of the most important tasks to do when you first take control of your budget.

Tip #5: Partner with other departments.

One of the biggest mistakes that many activity directors make is to rely completely and exclusively on their own budget. Since so much money is being cut from funds, now's the best time to begin to develop relationships with other departments, so that you will be in a position to co-host events.

For instance, if you are doing a career service related program, partner with career services. If you are doing a program for high achieving academic students, perhaps partner with the honors program.

Here's a list of potential partners on your campus:

- Residence Life
- Career Services
- Honors Program
- ROTC
- Alumni Association
- Faculty
- Dining Services
- Housing Services
- Diversity and Multicultural Office
- Commuter Services
- Student Leadership Programs
- Religious Services/Programs
- Study Aboard
- Academic Advisement
- Continuing Education
- Service Learning

Tip #6: Utilize your entire budget by the year's end.

One of the biggest mistakes that many professionals make when working with their budget is that they don't exhaust their entire budget. The reason to exhaust your entire budget is because often, when you don't spend the money, it gives the university justification to not allocate the same amount of money the following year.

By all means, exhaust all of your money before the year's end. Don't give any money back, because if you do, you may find that your funding is cut the following year, forcing you to cut programs that you are accustomed to doing.

Tip #7: Hold fundraisers.

If your budget has been slashed, one option is to organize fundraisers. I'm not talking about selling Girl Scout cookies, but fundraisers that students really can buy into and are willing to support. For example, most fundraisers that students are willing to support are those that entice other friends to bring in their friends.

A great idea for a fundraiser may be to have a student produced concert, a talent show or a fashion show.

You may decide that you want to put some of the proceeds towards a charitable cause. Taking this direction may be a great way to fund some of your smaller events.

Also, be very upfront about how you intend to spend your money and where the money is going, because you don't want to get in a situation where your intentions could be considered unethical.

Things to Consider

1. What system do you currently have in place to help organize your budget? If this

is your first time, who could you ask for advice about organizing your budget?

2. What portion of your budget do you have complete control over?

3. Write three things that you can do immediately to minimize your budget.

   a)

   b)

   c)

4. What could you do to reduce the hassles and obstacles to getting what is needed?

5. Who or what departments can you partner with in order to reduce your expenses?

CHAPTER 2

Motivating Unenthusiastic Student Leaders

"A man can succeed at almost anything for which he has unlimited enthusiasm." Charles M. Schwab

One of the challenges you never really expect to face is to motivate students who are supposedly there to motivate and inspire their peers. But quite commonly, sometimes this is a task you must perform as part of your job responsibilities.

In this chapter, I discuss details on how to better motivate students, and ways for a better understanding of how to help them become better student leaders and ambassadors of your program or office.

Tip #1: Find Out Why.

Sometimes we overlook the fact that students are given a lot to do when they come to campus. In order to really understand what gets them going and what motivates them, we sometimes have to play psychologist and figure out what makes them tick.

If you can find out why a student is unmotivated, or better yet, what gets them motivated, then you won't have to worry about explaining how to do an assignment, because they will already have the desire to make it happen.

Take the time to get to know the students and find out why (or why not) they are motivated. This can prove very beneficial as you go through your school year.

Tip #2: Process of elimination.

Sometimes the position that the student is in is not necessarily a good fit for them, nor is it a good use of their time. As a result, this requires you to make a tough decision and ask a student to either step down, or have them do something a bit different that will better utilize their gifts and talents. As long as your approach comes from a place of care and concern, then it will work out.

As a supervisor and mentor, one of your duties is to find ways to motivate your students to be their best and to bring out the best in them. But if all else fails, then you need to ask them to step down and allow another student to serve in that position.

It might be the most beneficial thing that you do, because one bad apple can ruin the whole bunch, and you don't want that. So use your best judgment.

Tip #3: Hire an expert or motivational speaker to tackle tough issues.

One of the many benefits of hiring an expert is that they can assist in some of those tough discussions, or they can facilitate tough discussions that either you may not have the time to do, or you may not want to do.

Hiring an expert or a motivational speaker saves you face, while allowing at least some of your message to be reinforced by way of someone else. And often when someone else does it, it is taken very differently than when you do it. So take advantage of this great opportunity and hire an expert or motivational speaker.

Tip #4: Provide student peers with more responsibility.

Often, it's other students who can give their fellow students a "kick in the pants" to motivate them better than you can. Nothing is more powerful than the power of peer influence, simply because peers tend to listen more to their peers than to administrators they can't relate with. So utilize peers or other high-achieving student leaders who can help to motivate other students.

Tip #5: Get to know their love language.

In Gary Chapman's book, *The Five Love Languages*, he talks about the 5 different ways we both express and receive love through the 5 love languages. They are:

1. Words of Affirmation
2. Quality Time
3. Receiving Gifts
4. Acts of Services
5. Physical Touch

Every student is motivated by one of these more than the others. Your job is to find out which one applies to them and how you can infuse their love language with their appreciation preference, so that you can use it to motivate them.

In doing so, you will have a better opportunity to motivate students and inspire them to do their best, so they can better serve their campus community.

Tip #6: Reward good acts.

Some students may just need a pat on the back, or for someone to say to them, "You are doing a great job today." Even though time is always limited, find ways to say, "Thank you." You also need to find ways to reward good acts, because when you reward a good act, it goes a long, long way.

Tip #7: Design a personal plan for each student leader.

This may take a little bit of work, but if you help them design a plan, or at least ask the right questions so they can begin to design their own plan, it will keep them interested and motivated, because they're doing something they are interested in and enjoy doing.

I had to do this quite a bit when I was supervising residence assistants in a previous job. In most cases it worked, because the students had a vested interest in what I was trying to get them to do, and they were able to personalize the responsibility they were given. Doing this will help you to get more from them, and they will get more out of the experience as well, because they will own it.

Tip #8: Create community standards to ensure accountability.

Nothing works better for a group of students than group accountability in the form of community standards. Community standards are nothing more than a strategy used to get everyone to buy into similar things everyone wants to see happen; for example, similar goals, similar interests, similar behaviors, or whatever situation exists.

When using community standards, have the students articulate what those community standards will be, and then hold them account-able. For instance, at the beginning of the school year, ask them what their expectations are, not only of you, but also of themselves. From there, have them begin to follow through with the commitments that they have established.

The key is that they are deciding on their value system, and you aren't the one forcing them to buy into your standards. Rather, they create it for themselves.

Tip #9: Weekly reward.

A colleague had a weekly reward system, where he awarded students for exceptional acts of kindness; things they did to support one another, and exceptional things they did that went above and beyond the job. He called the award the "Student Super Heroes in Training."

It worked, because it gave students the incentive to continue to do better and to go out of their way to do so. Remember, a little bit of recognition can go a long, long way.

Tip #10: Listen.

Sometimes we're so busy giving orders that we don't take time to listen to the people we're giving those orders to. This can be a challenge for many people, especially when you're talking about being tight on time.

When you take the time to listen to your supervisees and students, you find out a lot about them, as well as learn a lot about yourself. So it's best to take an opportunity to listen to them and see how their advice or their opinions can help you with the entire process.

Things to Consider

1. How can you structure your day-to-day events to be less administrative and more student centered?

2. List five forms of positive reinforcement you can provide for your student leaders.

   a)

   b)

   c)

   d)

   e)

3. What student leaders in your organization have the most influence? How can you use that to your benefit?

CHAPTER 3

Dealing with "Difficult" Students Leaders

"There is more hunger in this world for love and appreciation than for bread." Mother Teresa

We all encounter people in life that we are not so excited about working with, and because we deal with a lot of people in our line of work, unfortunately, sometimes these people are the very students we are here to serve.

What do you do when dealing with "difficult" student leaders? This chapter gives you tips to help you develop better relationships with "difficult" student leaders.

Tip #1: Get to the root of the problem.

Some students are upset and "difficult" because there is something going on in their life. You don't always understand what's going on in their life until you have a chance to get to the root of the problem. Before you pass judgment, take time to get to the root of the student's problem. This not only gives you more insight, but also an opportunity to make a real difference in their life. Remember, they don't know how much you care until you show them.

Tip #2: Is it really your students, or is it you?

Often, we hold other people to a much higher standard than we hold ourselves. It is not always necessarily the student's fault. Some-times we have to take a long, hard look at ourselves before we judge others. So before you say that the students are difficult, look at yourself first, and only then make an assessment of them.

Tip #3: Take time to get to know the students.

One of the best ways to get to know students is simply by asking them general questions, and then as time goes by, making an honest attempt to ask them questions that are a bit more personal.

Students want advisors they feel they can trust and that they know. In order to be that person, you must delve into their lives, obviously with their permission. But you must get to know who they are, what they're dealing with, and what their hopes and dreams may be. Once you better understand them, you will be in a much better position to work with your students.

One thing that I found very helpful in getting to know students was simply taking them out to lunch and spending time with them in a more comfortable situation where they could have a bit of downtime just to be themselves.

If possible, take them out to lunch/dinner, or somewhere outside of your work environment, and put them in a situation where you're not necessarily seen as their supervisor or the person in charge.

Tip #4: Show them that you care.

As stated previously (page 22), in his book *The Five Love Languages*, Gary Chapman explains the 5 ways people express their affection. Again, they include:

1. Words of Affirmation
2. Quality Time
3. Receiving Gifts
4. Acts of Services
5. Physical Touch

This book was intended for couples, but what's great about it is that it gives you an opportunity to gain insight into how to better serve the people that you work with. If you can figure out a person's love language, you can better motivate, serve, and acknowledge.

If you show people that you care, you have a much greater opportunity not only to get to know them better, but also to get them to be more productive in whatever task you set for them. It's all about relationships and showing that you care.

Tip #5: Give them a timeline.

At the very beginning, you must be crystal clear about your expectations of the students and, to some degree, what will happen to them if these expectations are not met.

Now, I'm not saying you should micro manage or be a drill sergeant, but it's essential to clearly communicate your expectations from the very beginning. If you don't, they will never be met. Your students will just go on with what they think is right.

On the other hand, if you give them a clear expectation about what you desire from them, it will increase your chances of reducing conflict. If there is conflict, then they know upfront how you plan to handle it and understand the consequences.

Tip #6: Ask them what *they* want from this experience.

One of the biggest questions that most supervisors fail to ask their supervisees is what *they* want out of it. What do they personally want to get out of this experience? This may seem like common sense, but it's not always common practice. Therefore, students and advisors must understand what they're getting out of this deal.

- Are they doing this because they want to earn money?
- Are they doing this because they want to put it on their résumé?
- Are they doing this because they are intrigued by it?

- Are they doing this because they want to be in a position of power?

There is a myriad of reasons why students choose to get involved on campus. It's your job to help them get what they want from the experience. From there, it should be a little easier to know how to motivate them and also remind them of their reasons for doing it.

For some students, it's just not worth it. But when you know their reasons, it gives you a better opportunity to incentivize the students, as well as keep them motivated and interested.

Tip #7: Every moment is a teachable moment.

This tip is not just for the student, but also for you. It's not all about the student learning from you; you also can learn a lot. In your role, you're not just the teacher, but also the learner. When students disappoint you or seem difficult to work with, ask yourself what you can learn from the situation. How can this situation make you a better advisor, mentor, and supervisor?

Undoubtedly, you may see this personality type or this situation again in your professional career, and knowing how to deal with it the first time will greatly diminish your chances of having to deal with it a second time. At the very least, it will provide a valuable lesson on how to deal with it the next time around.

Tip #8: Don't take it personally.

As servant leaders, we often wear our hearts on our sleeves and, as a result, probably take many things much more personally than we should. It's hard not to, because we put a lot of care into our job.

Sometimes students are dealing with much deeper issues that predate your relationship with them, or they are dealing with bigger issues that you may not necessarily even know about. Although, they're coming to your campus with history, it's an opportunity for you to help them become better people.

If there is a misunderstanding along the way, don't take it personally, because when you do, you lose the opportunity to improve their lives as well as yours.

Tip #9: Set expectations, but don't be disappointed if they're not met.

It's great to set expectations; however, students are going to make mistakes. They are going to do things that are contrary to your advice, and they are not always going to do things in character.

Remember, they are still going through the process of learning how to be who they will eventually become. And while it's very beneficial to set clear expectations, don't be disappointed or judgmental when they don't meet those expectations.

Tip #10: Don't single them out.

This may seem like common sense, but everyone has a different philosophy about how to motivate students or how they want to discipline students. Two of the worst ways to discipline a student are to single them out and to just give up on them.

Many of these students have had people in their past, and possibly their present, to give up on them. You are one of the few people that may have an opportunity to reach them, and the easiest ways to lose that opportunity to connect with them, and meet them in a space where you can affect change, are by singling them out or dismissing them.

One of the most underrated aspects of your job is to find ways to connect with students, so that you can bring them on board with your vision and help nurture them into being better people.

Things to Consider

1. Name three things that bring out the best in you. What triggers this emotion?

   a)

   b)

   c)

2. Name three things that bring out the worst in you. What triggers this emotion?

   a)

   b)

   c)

3. If you are having trouble communicating with a particular student leader or student leaders, who can you utilize to help facilitate your message?

CHAPTER 4

What's It To You?

Supervising, Advising, and Mentoring Student Leaders

"If your actions inspire others to dream more, learn more, do more and become more, you are a leader."
John Quincy Adams

In your position you are asked to wear many hats: parent, psychologist, the bad cop, academic advisor, and anything else that is needed at the time. However, there are no hats more often used than those of supervisor, advisor, and mentor. At times, you may be asked to wear more of one and less of the others, depending on the situation. It's about knowing when to wear each one and the differences between them.

In this section, we explore the roles of supervisor, advisor and mentor, what it means to be each, and some tips for helping make whichever role you take on at any particular time work for both you and the student.

Supervisor

When you hear the word *supervisor*, what comes to mind? Do you think of your first boss at your first job? Was it a young, cool supervisor who let you get away with things, or was he or she a micromanaging, stand-over-your-shoulder type?

Have you considered your own style of supervision? If so, what kind of supervisor are you? Was this the type you always aspired to be, or did it just happen that way?

You will develop your own style, but the real question is, "Will your style be influenced by your own experiences or the institution or organization that you work for?" It's a question of ownership. Here are a few tips to help you be a better supervisor.

Tip #1: Once is a habit.

There's a saying from one of my previous supervisors that "once is a habit." He was talking about the importance of nipping things in the bud before they become a problem.

As a supervisor, you should try your best to stop negative behaviors, actions and attitudes before they start, because if you don't address an undesirable behavior or comment at the outset, it will be an uphill battle to correct it down the road. So before you allow a negative behavior to affect your desired outcome, correct it in the beginning.

Tip #2: Play fair.

When working with students, the key is to remain consistent. What you do for one you must do for all, because if you are not consistent, your integrity will be compromised. As a supervisor, it's the one thing that gives you leverage. When your integrity is compromised, you are no longer in charge, because no one will respect you for the right reasons.

Tip #3: It's not you, it's your perception.

It's human nature to want to be liked. However, when you are striving to be liked by your staff, without a doubt, you will do things that rub some of your students the wrong way.

The sad fact about this is that it's not always your decision. Whenever you work for an institution, generally speaking, you must always put the organization or institution's interests ahead of your own, and sometimes even that of the students. While this may affect others' perceptions of you, you must do your best to not take it personally if others perceive your actions as synonymous with being a bad person.

Tip #4 One-on-one time.

Whenever you are afforded an opportunity to spend time with your students one-on-one, remember to use this time wisely. Their view of you is already on edge because of how they perceive you. The best thing you can do is to change your environment. Instead of having one-on-one meetings in your office, consider hosting them in the cafeteria or off-campus. This will remove some of the formality, which should put your supervisee at ease, and hopefully allow you to connect with them on a deeper level.

Tip #5: It's all in the lesson.

Don't be so hard on yourself. Whatever mistakes or misfortunes you experience should always be looked at as an opportunity to grow. If this is your first time, please remember that you are still learning the position and your own supervisory style.

Tip #6: You are a supervisor, not a dictator.

At some point after securing a supervisory position, most of us have at least thought about abusing our power. I know I did. But you are not paid to be a dictator. The biggest complaint that most supervisees give when they don't like their supervisor is that they are too involved with what they are doing and are bossy.

In the eyes of the supervisor, however, it looks different, because they feel as if they are working very hard. Be sure to balance your time at events, in your meetings, and in doing administrative work (and be seen doing it).

Tip #7: Don't forget to say thanks.

Here's a simple idea; find ways to say thanks. <u>Hint</u>: It doesn't always have to be monetary or tangible. Remember that the reason you are able to excel in your position is because of the cast members around you. Take time to say thanks, and you will be surprised at how far your "thank you" goes.

Advisor

As an advisor, you are commonly deferred to when you oversee an organization. You are there to advise. You are not there to over-manage. Rather, you are there to protect and shield your organization from costly mistakes through your words of wisdom, to help generate ideas, and if nothing else share your time, expertise and resources. You are an advisor.

Tip #1: Put all of your expectations on the table.

Be very clear about what you can and can't deliver. For many advisors, with the exception of academic advisors, it is not a full-time job. In many cases, this is a responsibility in addition to your full-time position. Therefore, it is very important that you know what to expect from the students and they know what to expect from you. If you don't communicate these expectations, your disappointment as well as theirs will be a foregone conclusion.

Tip #2: It's the little things, too.

Since being an "advisor" is usually an additional responsibility, don't create more work for yourself than is necessary. Utilize your talents to help your students, but remember that sometimes your presence alone is good enough. Sometimes just attending and supporting events is all that students want.

Tip #3: Be encouraging.

No matter what ideas your students bring to you, try your best to be encouraging, since in most cases you've been there. It's important to encourage them and to get them to look at things from as many different perspectives as possible, so that they can make good decisions.

Tip #4: Taking over an organization.

When you are asked to advise an organization that has been previously handled by another advisor, don't be so quick to change things until you gain their trust. This can be tricky, because as you are stepping in as a new advisor, some students may try to take advantage of your naïveté.

The institution, or your supervisor, may also have different ideas in mind and want you to be the person to carry them out. In these situations, it's best to include students in the decision as much as possible, so that they feel like they have a voice.

It is also helpful for you to gain as much clarity as possible regarding the situation from your institution and/or supervisor. This way, you can make an informed decision, one that will hopefully benefit those who are most affected.

Tip #5: Starting an organization.

Here's the scenario: You are in your office one day, and a group of students approaches you about wanting to start an organization. If you've never done this before, what do you do? The most logical first step would be to come up with a game plan that helps make this happen. Here are a few questions you may want to ask the group:

1. What is the organization?
2. What's your organization's mission?
3. How will it be structured? Do you have a constitution?
4. Do you already have interested members?
5. What role are you asking the advisor to play?
6. Why do you think this campus needs this organization?
7. What's your timeline for creating and activating this organization?
8. What kinds of events/activities will this organization sponsor?

9. How are you different from other organizations?
10. Do you have a co-advisor in mind?

Without a doubt, there are other important questions that you will need to ask, and it's very important for you to ask the right questions before you make a commitment and/or help to approve the organization.

Mentor

Webster defines the word *mentor* as a wise or trusted adviser or guide. Mentoring is a great way to connect with students on a much deeper level. It's also a great way to give back. However, mentoring is completely optional.

Mentoring can be, and often is, time-consuming, which is the reason most people don't do it. It also often requires a long-term commitment from both the mentor and mentee.

Tip #1: Set boundaries.

It is important to set boundaries at the start, since you will possibly have very intimate conversations and interactions. You may truly care about a student, but you also must be aware of how your caring or a relationship could be perceived by others at your school.

Sadly, even at the best institutions, there are instigators, gossips, and the like. The last thing you need in your profession is a jaded perception that ultimately affects your career. Therefore, set boundaries, not just for your own protection, but for that of the student.

Tip #2: Know when to say "No."

As a mentor, your job is not to agree with everything. Your job is to help guide the student in the many aspects of their life that go beyond both the classroom and campus. Don't be afraid to disagree, but at the same time be willing to explain your position.

Tip #3: Listen up!

As a mentor, your greatest gift to your mentee is sometimes your willingness to listen. Most people just want to be heard; so make listening a big part of your relationship, and you will always be in a better position to guide your mentee.

Tip #4: Be consistent.

Once you determine what you can and cannot do, be consistent. For instance, if you wish to meet once a week, then meet once a week. Do what you can, but be consistent in whatever you do.

Tip #5: Leverage your relationships.

As a mentor, you are probably better connected to your institution than the student. Understand that you are not the be-all and end-all, but that given your connections, you can refer them to colleagues to help them get connected and have a chance to develop relationships. This will also show them how to do it for others.

Tip #6: What is right isn't always popular, what is popular isn't always right.

There will be times when you may have to do things in the student's best interest that they may not agree with. It's okay, as long as it is ultimately what's best for them, because they don't have the experience you have and, therefore, don't possess your insight.

Things to Consider

1. What words best describe your supervisory style, your advisory style, and your mentoring style?

   a)

   b)

   c)

2. If you had to choose between supervising, advising and mentoring, what role are you most comfortable with? Why?

3. List two possible campus or community resources that can help each of your student leaders. How will these campus resources help them resolve the current challenges they face?

   a)

   b)

CHAPTER 5

Getting Faculty and Staff Cooperation

"There is no such thing as a self-made man. You will reach your goals only with the help of others."
George Shinn

Did you know that your greatest assets on a college campus are the colleagues that you see and work with every day? The reason they are such a great asset is because they have access to resources you may not necessarily be aware of. Also, they can help you come up with some very good and creative ideas to help you improve your job performance and also serve your students.

This chapter covers tips on how to get faculty and staff on board with some of your initiatives, programs, and events.

Tip #1: It is all about relationships.

If you were to go to a complete stranger and ask if they would volunteer for you, their answer would probably be no. Of course, this would depend on how you ask and what is in it for them. My point is that when asking for favors, it's important to have relationships with the people you are asking for their help.

One of the best ways to start a relationship with someone is to be intentional about the type of relationship you want to enter. Now, I'm not saying that you need to be friends with everyone you have a working relationship with, but it's important for you to know them well enough, so that when the time comes for you to ask them for favors, you can do just that.

Relationships are key in making sure that you get faculty and staff cooperating. So get out of your comfort zone. Get out of your office from time to time and get to know some of the colleagues on your campus. It will serve you well in your time at your university.

Tip #2: Showcase their expertise.

There is nothing better or more significant for a faculty member than to talk about their own area of interest, their hobbies, or their research. By all means, identify faculty who can help you achieve your goals, and then showcase their expertise.

For example, maybe you are doing a program for Earth Day, or World AIDS Day, or Martin Luther King, Jr. Day. Try to identify a faculty member's interest and match it to the event. This will give you a more likely chance that they will assist you in whatever projects you want them to do.

Maybe you need a faculty member to talk about their research for an upcoming lunch and learn series, or a movie and discussion program. This is a great opportunity to showcase their expertise, because, again, this is something they are very interested in doing anyway. Please note when asking them, don't make it hard for them to showcase their expertise, and don't turn it into some type of research project for them.

Tip #3: Come from a place of service.

This is very important, because when you ask for favors, you want to be the first to extend your services to them. For example, you may say, "If you ever need a proctor for an exam, I'm your person," or, "If you need a guest speaker for your class, let me know."

It just depends on what they need from you, but if you come from a place of service, you will always have an opportunity to get the things you want. As legendary motivational speaker Zig Ziglar said, "You can get anything you want out of life if you help enough people get what they want."

Tip #4: Go to lunch with them.

One of the easiest ways that I got to know many of my colleagues on campus was simply going to lunch with them, spending time with them, and figuring out what they want out of a relationship or what makes them happy, and going from there. It doesn't cost much, but the dividends will pay off greatly, if you continue to nurture the relationship.

Tip #5: Understand why it is important.

Convincing people to understand why what you do is important sometimes can be daunting and even downright scary, but it's very necessary to do so if you truly believe in what you do. You are the biggest advocate for your cause.

The reason why convincing faculty members to support your event is so important is because they are the only group that can "mandate" students to attend an event. So be sure to explain to them why your events are important and why their involvement is paramount. After all, when your goals are consistent, it shouldn't be a problem for you to explain why you need their help

Tip #6: Don't ask for too much.

Although I'm advocating you should ask for help, you don't want to ask for too much; at least, not too soon. Like most members in the institution, faculty members are very busy; therefore, you must keep in mind their schedules and commitments. They are not only pro-fessionals, but they also have lives outside the university, so don't ask them for much. Instead, try to make their involvement seamless.

For example, maybe ask them to judge a particular contest, or request them to provide a lecture or talk they have already presented. Again, don't ask for too much, because quite frankly, you may scare them off.

Tip #7: Don't forget to say thank you.

Many of the people who will assist you in your goals of building your relationship with students and putting on great events don't have to do it. It is not in their job requirement. Usually, certain staff and faculty members are not required at all to do anything outside of their own research or teacher responsibilities.

It's very important that you find ways to say thank you, and it doesn't necessarily have to be extensive. It can be a nice voicemail. It can be a nice card. It can be praise to their supervisor, a thank you card, taking them out for lunch, a small gift, or words of encouragement. It could be anything. Be as creative as you want to be, but whatever you do, don't forget to say thank you.

Tip #8: Find out their level of interest.

Most people will be willing to help you if they are interested in what you're offering in the first place. At a previous university I created faculty dinners. When I first introduced these get-togethers, I emailed all the professors I had access to and simply asked a question, "Would you be interested in eating with the students and talking about your research or a topic that interests you?"

This proved to be very helpful. I found that over 80% of the faculty members were interested in participating in this type of event, because it had never been done before, and it gave them an opportunity to really get to know students on a much more intimate level.

You never know until you ask, but when you do ask, make sure you get some type of preliminary email or message out there to help generate interest in what you are trying to do.

Things to Consider

1. Identify the people you should get to know. What could you do to help them before asking for anything in return?

2. What do you think are the major reasons why many faculty and staff members choose not to get involved with students on campus? How can you change this?

CHAPTER 6

Marketing Standing Room Only Events

"If you can imagine it, you can achieve it; if you can dream it, you can become it." William Arthur Ward

Every meeting planner's dream is to have a fun, memorable, productive and well-attended event. Unfortunately, sometimes common mistakes that can be avoided prevent this from happening. In this chapter, I discuss some of the common mistakes that activity coordinators make when planning and marketing events.

Mistake #1: Planning an event at the last minute.

There is nothing more disastrous than planning an event at the last minute. For one thing, it puts you in a rush mode and makes you look bad if it's not executed well. Most events that are planned at the last minute don't turn out well, because there's not enough time for all of the coordination that's involved. To avoid this, make sure to plan your event well in advance. It helps if you delegate tasks to others beforehand.

Mistake #2: One stream of marketing.

Gone are the days when you need to rely on only one way to market an event. Use all resources available to you, like social media, fliers, word of mouth, direct mail, emails, and bribery. Whatever you need to use, use it, but don't just rely on one way to market an event. Use multiple venues to market to a targeted group, because people forget about events as time goes on. Make sure you have a good marketing plan that starts weeks in advance and, of course, on the day of the event.

Mistake #3: Having too high expectations.

One of the biggest mistakes people make in marketing is the idea that their event is somehow superior to other events. Having too high expectations can discourage you and your students, and you can come away with very low morale. Make sure you are on an even keel, and that you don't have unrealistic expectations of the event, because whether it's well or poorly attended, you can take away a teachable moment.

Mistake #4: Timing.

This was one of my biggest mistakes when I was planning events as a college student and also as a leader. I was often unaware of other events that were happening. Make sure that you are in tune with your school's calendar and those of other clubs, and what they're doing at the same time as your event. Timing is everything in planning events, and poor timing can cost you the attendance and the outcome that you desire.

Mistake #5: Not getting student or faculty buy-in.

This is a killer, simply because when you're planning an event, you want to make sure that people attend. The people who will be attending are your students, so make sure that this is something they are interested in doing.

One of the most popular events I did was a chili cook-off. In order for me to get student and faculty buy-in, I got them to participate by making their own chili recipes. In addition, it was a competition. Always make sure that you are getting student and faculty buy-in.

Mistake #6: Doing all the marketing yourself.

I cannot overemphasize how big a mistake this is. As an activities coordinator, you cannot do it all by yourself, so having a group of people to assist you with marketing the event will help you greatly increase the marketability of your events, and perhaps the attendance.

Mistake #7: Your title isn't provocative enough.

When planning events, make sure that you use catchy event titles. Use titles that are provocative and will be memorable, but that also will get students interested in coming. You want them to understand that if they don't attend, they are missing out on a huge opportunity.

Mistake #8: Not providing incentives.

Students are very busy and don't come to events unless their friends invite them, or unless there's food or some type of prize involved. Don't be afraid to give students incentives. Whatever it takes to lure the students, you should be willing to do it. Provide them with incentives that they will find useful.

Mistake #9: Unwillingness to try different things.

There is no perfect formula for getting students to come to your events. There will be times when you have to experiment a bit to figure out what works and what doesn't. Be sure that you try different things, because if events are predictable or boring, the word will get out. Be willing to try things that are out of the box, unusual, and things that will help people make the decision easy to attend.

Mistake #10: Having events that are boring.

Think about it; students have been in class all day, and the last thing they want to do is go to an energy draining event that no one wants to attend. Make sure that your events are not only fun, but also relevant to whatever they may be going through. Timing is very important, but relevance is even more important, as well as making sure that the students have fun. It gets students coming back to your events time and time again.

Mistake #11: Not collecting students' information at events.

This is very important, because the people who attend your event will probably be the very same people who attend your future events.

Like all good marketing strategies, you must continue to market to those people you already know have a vested interest in your services. Don't forget to collect their information and stay in touch by giving your students access to the latest news about your events to keep them coming. It will help you to build attendance and also create an incentive for them to bring a friend the next time they come to your event.

Things to Consider

1. How can you create a greater awareness of a difficult issue on your campus?

2. List 5-10 marketing techniques that you currently utilize to promote your events. What's working? What's not working?

a)

b)

c)

d)

e)

3. What other offices and departments can help you promote your campus events?

4. How do you plan to use your students' talents and skills to help you promote your events?

CHAPTER 7

Organizing Student Conferences

"If everyone is moving forward together, then success takes care of itself." Henry Ford

Most schools hold conferences biannually or once a year, usually in the spring. Whether this is your first time doing a conference or you are a seasoned veteran, this chapter covers some of the basics for organizing a conference, with time-saving tips to help you ensure great turnout at your conference and the desired results.

Tip #1: Decide on a theme.

One of the first decisions you must make when designing a conference is why you want to do the conference in the first place.

- What are your reasons for hosting this conference?
- Are you hosting this conference to address a specific problem on your campus?
- Are you planning it because it is expected every year?
- Are you targeting a specific group?

In most cases, advisors are asked to help organize student leadership conferences, multi-culture conferences and others geared towards solving a problem or tackling a university initiative. In any event, you must know at the outset why you are doing it and decide on a theme.

Tip #2: Assemble a committee.

It is impossible to organize an entire conference all by yourself. If you try, you will find it very difficult. When planning a conference, it is important to determine who will serve on your committee and what their responsibilities will be.

- Who will be responsible for marketing the conference?
- Who will be responsible for registration?
- Who will be responsible for organizing the workshops?
- Who will approve the workshops?
- Who will be responsible for the assessment and evaluation of the conference?

Your conference will only be as good as the committee you appoint to help you conduct it, so make sure you choose wisely.

Tip #3: How will you assess or evaluate your conference?

This is very important, because many conferences have room for improvement. You will know where improvements can be made only if you take the time to design an effective way to assess the conference. Also, you must ask yourself when the appropriate time would be to assess or evaluate the conference.

- How exactly will you assess your conference?
- Will you make an assessment after every workshop?
- Will you get feedback from delegates after the conference via email or through an online service, such as Survey Monkey?

The results will depend largely on what areas you want to assess and the information you hope to gather from the conference.

Tip #4: Get volunteers.

Your committee must have enough people who are willing to donate their time to help you make the conference go as smoothly as possible.

- Who will these volunteers be and exactly what will they do?
- Will these volunteers be students?

- Will they be your campus colleagues?
- Will you have them working at the registration table?
- Will they be presenting workshops at your conference?
- Will you have them setting up?
- Will you have them cleaning up?

However you use them, your conference will run much smoother if you have volunteers. Don't forget to always give them something at the end to show your appreciation.

Tip #5: Acquire vendors.

Do you want your vendors to be sponsors, or do you want to offer them the opportunity to advertise, sell their products and services while they are there?

If you plan to use vendors as either speakers or entertainers, it's best to get them on board as soon as you come up with a theme. Get a signed contract from each vendor to secure the date. If they are not speakers or entertainers, make sure that you are very clear about what their responsibilities are and what they can expect from you.

- Do you want your vendors to be sitting at tables or have booths?
- Do the vendors have their own insurance?
- Do you want them to donate some of the door prizes?
- Do you want them to fund some of your other expenses in return for exposure and advertising?

These are all questions you need to ask when deciding upon vendors.

Tip #6: Entertainment.

Let's say you want to have music at your conference. This can be done either through a DJ or a PA system. It's really up to you and depends on what you want. Think about the timing of it, when you want to have it, and the type of music you want to be played. Not everyone has the same taste in music, so be very thoughtful about the music selection.

Tip #7: How will you market this event?

An event can be marketed in several ways. You can use traditional methods like fliers and word of mouth, as well as social media, emails, and many other venues. The key to maximizing your marketing efforts is to target them towards a specific group of people and make sure that you constantly talk about the event.

Also, make sure that everyone is aware of the venue and that the campus supports it, so that it is advertised everywhere. The best people to help you advertise are those who care about it the most; your committee and others involved in the process. So make sure that you have the right marketing tools to guarantee that that happens.

Tip #8: Incentives for attending.

Your incentives should be attractive to your attendees. Maybe you're offering things like pens, pencils, backpacks or t-shirts. No matter what the incentives are, they will certainly add to the allure of coming to the conference.

Another creative idea includes giving them coupon books for businesses in your local area. If it's a regional conference, this works very well in partnership with the local businesses and vendors in your area. If it's a local conference, you may still want to bring in local businesses and vendors. It helps everyone involved.

Yet another incentive is to make sure that the event provides useful information for your attendees. Nothing is worse than having a conference where no one gets anything out of it. Don't just have a conference for the sake of having it. Instead, have plenty of good content that your attendees can take away and use soon, right after the conference.

Tip #9: Organizing workshops, presenters.

Organization is key, because certain details must be coordinated behind the scenes. A very important question to consider is who your presenters will be.

- Who will your presenters be?
- Will they be volunteers, faculty, or other colleagues and staff members?
- Will they be people from outside your school?
- Who will provide the equipment?
- Will presenters be mandated to bring their own screens, laptops and projectors, or will you provide them?

Here's a checklist to help you stay organized for a successful event.

- Nominate one person to be in charge of making sure that the presenters have everything together.

- Include your AV person in this process to make sure that someone is working on the day of the event, especially if it's on a weekend, and to make sure the equipment is available for that particular day.
- Give presenters a deadline for submitting their proposals. Typically, you want that to be at least 3-4 weeks prior to your conference; that way, you have ample time to organize the conference in the best possible way to include all details.
- Make sure that the presenters provide you with workshops and breakout sessions that are interesting, new, and provocative.

Tip #10: How long do you want the conference to run?

How long you want the conference to be is an important question, because its length will determine almost everything else, in terms of the resources you need to make the event happen.

- Do you want it to be one day only?

- For two days, for three days, or a half-day?
- Will it be a drop-in type conference?

Tip #11: Lodging.

If the conference is held with the idea of attracting attendees from other areas, what type of lodging information will you provide for them? This is very important, because most people want to know where they can stay during the conference.

Talk to a local hotel and get special rates for your delegates to avoid asking them to pay a lot of money. It's also a good idea to have extra rooms in reserve, in the event you have late registration attendees.

Tip #12: Look to past conferences to see what made them a success.

If this is a conference that has been going on for several years at your institution or in your organization, look back at other conferences that worked well and were successful in the past, and learn from them. They might have a general outline that you can use. You can then modify certain items, such as the theme, to bring your particular flavor to the conference.

Tip #13: Pre-survey.

A pre-survey is very helpful, because it gives you an idea of what people are looking for. Maybe people can speak about past experiences of the same conference and tell you which parts they didn't enjoy. Maybe they want to have specific food served, or to know about specific issues that are new to their industry.

It is also helpful to pre-survey past attendees, because the information gives you a good idea of what to provide. It's a preliminary step, but most people who plan conferences make a huge mistake by not asking past attendees, as well as their target market, what they really want out of the conference.

Tip #14: Delegate.

Delegation is very important, because as a conference chair you cannot do it all by yourself. As the saying goes…in order to make the dream work, you must make the team work. So make sure that you're using all of your own resources to the maximum, but also taking the opportunity to delegate where needed.

Tip #15: Don't forget to say thank you.

Nothing is more draining or bad for morale as not being thanked or honored in some way for all the hard work someone put in. Take time to say "thank you" to your committee and all volunteers. Acknowledge them publicly in front of everyone at the beginning and/or the end of the conference in some type of special recognition. This way, they will be a lot more willing to help you out in future years as this conference continues.

Here is a **Summary of Steps** for a great conference:

- Determine theme, date and purpose of conference.
- Secure rain date.
- Secure funding, equipment, and the venue.
- Secure vendors and catering.
- Appoint your committee.
- Assign committee member tasks.
- Execute tasks and schedule regular conference check-in meetings.
- Market, market, market!
- Host conference.
- Reward your committee.
- Evaluate conference.

Things to Consider

1. What problems or concerns will your conference help address?

2. What help do you need to get the outcome you desire?

3. How many helpers are needed? How many are required?

CHAPTER 8

Assessing and Evaluating Events

"Getting things done is not always what is most important. There is value in allowing others to learn, even if the task is not accomplished as quickly, efficiently or effectively." R.D. Clyde

You can't improve on anything until you know exactly what needs to be improved. One of the challenges to creating better initiatives, programs and activities on campus is for you to evaluate what they are like. And in order to do so, you need to understand the importance of an evaluation and how to do it. Next we explore some ways and give tips on how to better assess the activities on your campus, and why you should assess them in the first place.

Tip #1: Get feedback.

Always have a feedback box present at your events, because it's a great way to get instant comments and opinions on them. Often we get egocentric about our events and how great they are, but we never know what the very people we are serving really think about them. A good way to get their opinion is to have a feedback box present at each event.

Tip #2: Focus groups.

Focus groups are not as difficult as you might think. Just have a set of questions available that you ask students. In fact, this is a time when you may want to involve your grad assistant. Also, if you are a grad assistant, this may be a good opportunity for you to do some of the work you want to do for your classes. By using focus groups, you can actually get qualitative data to help you improve some of your campus events.

Tip #3: Ongoing assessment.

Do an assessment at the beginning, middle, and end of the year. This will tell you where you need to make things happen. It will also quickly give you a recurring assessment of the current situation. This process gives you much more data on how to improve your campus the following year.

Tip #4: Seek help.

Ask researchers on your campus for assistance. Let's say you have a campus that is full of researchers, whereas another might be full of faculty members. Ask them what they have used to streamline their collection of data, as well as if they have a better way to evaluate events, programs and initiatives. You may be surprised at some of their ideas and methods, but it never hurts to ask. They may have a more systematic way of doing things that you can benefit from in this job, as well as in a future job.

Tip #6: Create easy assessments.

Make your assessment and evaluation forms easy to understand, so that people can give you actual details on an event, telling you exactly what they liked or disliked, as opposed to how well they liked the event on a scale of 1-5. And give sufficient room on the forms to explain.

Things to Consider

1. How do you currently evaluate your events?

2. When evaluating and assessing your events, do you also take an opportunity to get to know the issue?

3. How will the way you assess your events justify future funding of your events?

CHAPTER 9

Writing Learning Outcomes

"That is what learning is. You suddenly understand something you've understood all your life, but in a new way." Doris Lessing

These days, most funding on college campuses is tight, and they are under tight scrutiny with regard to budgets and fiscal responsibility. As a result, many departments and offices are being asked questions about learning outcomes, and they are required to articulate clearly what's being learned. In this chapter, we discuss tips on how to write clear and concise learning outcomes that will justify your initiatives, programs, and events.

Tip #1: Be clear and concise.

This is very important, because most people who write learning outcomes could use improvement in this area. The key question is: "What do you want students or your learners to take away from this particular event or initiative?" The clearer you are and the simpler you make this, the better. Simplicity is the key.

Tip #2: Just say it and correct mistakes later.

At one time in my career, I was asked to write learning outcomes on pretty much every-thing I wanted to do. I was very frustrated, because I wanted it to sound the way I thought about it, and most of the time it wasn't communicated that way. I had to learn how to just say it, and then go back and correct mistakes later.

At times, it required working with a colleague or my supervisor to make the wording clearer. After involving others, this process really minimized a lot of my frustration. So when you're writing a learning outcome, sometimes it's best just to get it all down, and then go back and edit it later.

Tip #3: Justify it.

The success of writing a learning outcome depends on your ability to justify why an event or initiative is important. When I'm writing learning outcomes for my own programs featured on my website, I typically give a description, but I also include the justification within the description.

It's helpful to know why you are writing a learning outcome in the first place. You can then use that as a departure point to explain what students are getting from it. Good phrases to use are the following; just fill in the blanks:

* "Students will learn how to…"
* "Learners will, upon going through this program or workshop…"
* "Learners will learn how to…."

Tip #4: Why are these outcomes important?

This is a critical question, because when writing a learning outcome, you always want to tie it in with a university initiative that they may ask you to provide. In fact, it's always important to bring in other factors that influence the learning outcomes.

For instance, if your institution has a college completion initiative they are working to achieve, it's important to tie your learning outcomes to that mission, being very clear and very goal-oriented about the language. This helps you to find the right words, even if it means including some of their mission or value statements in your learning outcomes.

Tip #5: Get help from experts.

By experts, I mean those professionals you plan to incorporate into your initiatives or programs. For example, if you are bringing in a speaker, that speaker or expert should be able to help you write a learning outcome.

Simply ask the speaker to write a quick summary of what their program is about and what students will gain as a result of the presentation. In doing so, it either gives you an idea of what to do or which direction you should go with yours.

Other experts to ask are campus researchers. There are many researchers or faculty members on campus with experience in writing learning outcomes, so it's best to ask them for assistance if possible.

Things to Consider

1. What current initiatives is your institution attempting to implement? What's your role in helping to make this happen?

2. What's your game plan for helping to address your school's new initiative?

94

CHAPTER 10

Transitioning Student Leaders

"Change always comes bearing gifts." Price Pritchett

One of the most important and essential keys to student leadership is the implementation of a student transition program. This oftentimes gets overlooked, because when students are elected, they are immediately thrust into their positions.

In order for your student leaders to be successful, you must find ways to help them transition into the position in a very smooth and effective manner. In this chapter, I provide solutions and tips to help facilitate that process.

Tip #1: Start early.

Start early: the sooner, the better. If you start the transition process as soon as elections are over, or just before elections, it will help in several different ways. Think about it; in most institutions, elections are held either in February or March, and as a result, new student leaders are inaugurated right before the school year ends. They could use the summer to plan for the fall, and some students don't do that.

When in the student leadership process, make sure that you start as early as possible; it will help you in the long run. It will also help students better learn how to work together as they go through the transition process.

Tip 2: Ask them what they want out of this experience.

Not every student leader wants the same thing. Some student leaders are in it because they want to build their résumé. Some are in it because they want to give back to their campus. Be very direct with your students, because it is better to spend your time training and cultivating student leaders who really want to give back.

It's very, very important for you to understand what they want from this experience, and then find ways to connect their goals with how you can help them.

Tip #3: Q & A luncheons.

This is a precursor for finding and identifying student leaders early on. Hosting this type of event is important, because it gives student leaders who aspire to go into elected positions an opportunity to ask some of those very important questions. On the other hand, for student leaders who are currently in a position, or who know that they want to go into a position, it gives them an opportunity to re-evaluate and also reaffirm leadership commitments.

Tip #4: Host a student leadership transition retreat.

Hosting a student leadership retreat gives incoming student leaders a chance to learn from incumbent campus leaders. Accordingly, this may be something that you can do as soon as they are elected, or shortly after.

In doing so, this gives them a chance to really get familiar with their job responsibilities, and an opportunity to ask other student leaders and graduating seniors some things they learned from being in a leadership position.

Tip #5: Plan a student leadership orientation.

If you decide to plan a student leadership orientation, it will give leaders an opportunity to get familiar with their campus environment, the resources, constitution, bylaws, and other important aspects of their new position. It works best to do this over the summer, when things slow down a bit.

Tip #6: Create a concise student leadership manual.

It's important to have some type of guideline for new student leaders, because many of them have never been a student leader before and don't know where to begin. One of the best things to do is to give them a handbook that they can reference time and time again.

This manual should contain important information, such as campus resources, a sample calendar of events, annual events, and answers to frequently asked questions.

When you provide a student leadership manual or guide, make sure that it is also covers basic information, like how to run meetings, how to plan events, and how to market events.

You can also create a leadership training video and may want to consider posting it online.

Tip #7: Utilize other student leaders in the transition process.

Perhaps you can start a mentoring program that begins earlier in the year to help identify student leaders interested in the position. A great idea is to implement a shadowing program.

When I was a resident assistant, we had a shadowing program for aspiring resident assistants. It was designed to help us get to know soon-to-be candidates better, and gave candidates an opportunity to see what the position was like.

This is very helpful to give them a better understanding of what they are getting themselves into, and maybe even how they can improve the process themselves.

Tip #8: Provide aspiring student leaders an increased amount of responsibility.

When you provide aspiring student leaders with a taste of what it's like to serve, you don't want to give them too much responsibility. However, you must give them enough responsibility, whereby they have an opportunity to learn all they need and want to know.

Tip # 9:   Provide them with reports from previous years or the current year.

Providing incoming student leaders with reports gives them the opportunity to see, in a very documented fashion, what has worked and what didn't work. It also gives them a blueprint for success. The saying goes that "success leaves clues," so lead your student leaders by helping them to transition, and model success, so that they may be effective in their position.

Tip #10:   Share challenges with them that you have experienced or are dealing with.

Don't just give your own perspective. Instead, get a group of previous and/or current student leaders to do a roundtable, where they can tell new leaders, "Here's what to watch out for," or, "This is how you should address this problem," because chances are that the new leaders will face similar challenges that previous student leaders faced.

Tip #11: Acquaint them with their new environment and key resources.

Acquainting student leaders with their new environment is critical, because you don't want their first day on the job to be unfamiliar. Think about it; whenever you started a new job, you probably had an orientation or some way to get acquainted with the people in your office. Give the newcomers a chance for that same advantage in their new situation to become familiar with the environment and key resources.

Tip #12: Provide them with all records.

Provide them with financial statements, the constitution, bylaws, meeting minutes and other reports, as well as everything possible to help them in their job.

<u>Caution</u>: Give them this information in increments, as you don't want to overwhelm them or scare them away. There is a lot to being a student leader, but the most important part is being aware of all key resources and information.

Tip #13: Include outgoing leadership in the process of transition.

Allow them to learn from previous mistakes and for other students who have been in their position to help guide them. Who is better for this than previous student leaders? Sometimes it's better to learn from history than personal experience. Give them added opportunities by including outgoing leadership in the process.

<u>Things to Consider</u>

1. How do you plan to utilize current student leaders to help transition incoming student leaders? List 5-10 strategies:

   a)

b)

c)

d)

e)

2. What events or activities would be helpful when orientating new student leaders?

3. What are the five most difficult challenges for students in a new position?

a)

b)

c)

d)

e)

CHAPTER 11

Running Elections

"This is not an election where we hand out gifts. It is an election where we ask everyone to contribute more."
Helle Thorning-Schmidt

One of the most important yearly events is student elections, as they will determine the future direction of where your organization may go. Particularly if you advise student government organizations, your role is critical in the organization's direction and what you might do.

It's important that you conduct an election process that is not only fair, but also open to anyone who wants to run. In this chapter, we cover tips to help you do just that.

Tip #1: Marketing.

I cannot emphasize enough how important marketing an election is, because if people don't know about it, they won't participate in the process. When you know exactly when the election will be and how you will determine the results, it's very important to market it in a way that will be of maximum benefit to your students.

Tip #2: Be bipartisan.

Never, ever, ever show favoritism during an election. It may be tempting to favor one student over another, but you never want to be in a position of being accused of showing favor. Remember, your job as an advisor is to advise during the process, not to determine the outcome. So leave that to the students who vote.

Tip #3: Utilize other campus colleagues.

If you don't have existing relationships with other colleagues on campus, this is a great time to begin building these relationships, because many of these colleagues will be happy to be part of a student election process. It gives them an opportunity to connect with students, and most importantly, it gives you an opportunity to build an alliance that helps you down the road.

Tip #4: Be clear about your expectations.

Be very clear about your expectations of campus colleagues and exactly what you want them to do regarding elections. Students should know exactly what the consequences are for their actions and also your expectations that there is a level of respect for each candidate and their opponent(s). Once you lay out these ground rules, it's much easier for students to know exactly what is expected.

Tip #5: Evaluate the old system.

Especially if this is your first time, it's very important to evaluate what was done in the past <u>before</u> elections. Perhaps something needs to be changed, or perhaps nothing needs to be changed, but one thing is for sure: Changes should only be made if they improve the election process, so that it is fair, balanced, and open to all who want to participate in the process.

Tip #6: Keep it clean.

Before things begin to get out of hand, you must nip things in the bud and be sure that everyone understands the consequences in cases of abuse, unfairness, or anything underhanded in the election process. The best way to ensure a good or successful election is to make sure that the expectation is for a clean election. Don't be afraid to step in as an advisor and let students know what your expectations are and how they are set forth.

Tip #7: Prequalify candidates.

I remember an embarrassing occurrence at my institution. A candidate was elected to the position of SGA president, but was later removed due to her grades. This could have been avoided if the advisor had just taken the time to check grades, disciplinary records, and other pertinent information for the candidates.

As an advisor, your job is to make sure that things go smoothly behind the scenes. It's one thing for the students to know that they are not qualified. It's quite another for the administration to not know that the student is not qualified for a leadership position.

Tip #8: Stay true to a system.

Student-run elections can sometimes get a bit complicated. Be sure that whatever system you decide to use, that you stay true to that system. Have a system in place that will allow you to keep things moving forward, regardless of the outcome and any interruptions that may happen, like inclement weather or other circumstances, a system robust enough that takes into account unforeseen challenges.

Tip #9: Encourage students to run, even if they are not visibly present.

Make sure that all students who want to run for office have an opportunity to do so or are encouraged to run; not just incumbent student leaders, but also students who may not be as actively involved on campus. As an advisor, make sure that these students are very aware that they are part of the electoral process.

Things to Consider

1. What would the ideal election look like for you? Describe in complete detail.

2. How will you attract and involve non-student leaders in the election process?

3. Is there a system or protocol in place in the event elections must be rescheduled?

4. How will you utilize technology in the election process?

CHAPTER 12

Leaving Your Mark
On Your School

"Effective people are not problem-minded; they're opportunity minded. They feed opportunities and starve problems." Stephan R. Covey

Part of your hope is that you have made a difference at your institution by the time you leave. Helpfully, you will know that your time was well-spent, and that somehow you impacted the lives of the very people you were asked to serve – your students.

Leaving your mark doesn't require you to stay there for 30 years or to put in place a program that has never been done before. But it does require you to be thoughtful and intentional about the things you do on campus. In this chapter, I present tips to help you leave a lasting legacy on your campus.

Tip #1: Create a System.

"What system or program do I want to put in place?" Asking yourself this question allows you an opportunity to figure out what you want to do, how you want to do it, and how to go about accomplishing a particular feat. Maybe you want to start a tournament that's never been done before, or a male mentoring program or other program that addresses a problem on campus. Whatever the goal, have clarity about why you are doing it and how you plan to put it in place.

Tip #2: Make sure you own it.

As a former employee at some of my institutions, I always made it a point to try my best to bring something unique to the campus, because I always knew this was a selling point for when I moved on to the next campus or university. It allowed me an opportunity to invent a program that had never been done before, one that I could talk about later in other interview situations and my consulting practices.

In whatever you do, make sure that your creation can be taken with you wherever you decide to go in your career, because more often than not, you will want to take it with you, and it belongs to you.

Tip #3: Build it like a tradition.

When you build something that's great and turn it into a tradition, the people who carry on your legacy are often people who have just as much invested in it as you do. I did quite a few programs at my previous campuses, from male mentoring programs to volleyball tournaments, to faculty dinners. In every instance, years after I left they continued, in part, because the energy transferred to people who were just as invested as I was and wanted to keep the tradition. Some programs became events that everyone wanted to be involved in and prepared for.

I have found that it's very helpful when speaking to competitions, such as a sports tournament among your office or department, people oftentimes want to improve upon your creation and make it even better.

Tip #4: Pass it off to someone you trust.

When doing an event, you want to pass it off to people that you know will be just as excited as you are about it. Rather than share your legacy, you want to put it in the hands of people you not only trust, but also people who will never, ever leave and will always be there.

I'm talking about the students. If you put it in the hands of the students, they will ensure that your legacy is carried on, especially if it's something they will get something out of or that they can buy into.

Things to Consider

1. If you could do one thing that would determine how you would like to be remembered on your campus, what would it be?

2. What current problems do you have the ability to resolve in your current position?

3. What professional goals do you plan to achieve in your current position this year?

4. What resources will you need to utilize in order to leave your mark on your school?

CHAPTER 13

Balancing Your Personal and Professional Life

"At times, it is difficult to keep a proper balance in our lives. But, over time, an improper balance will lead to problems." Catherine Pulsifer

As student affairs professionals, we often don't take the time to have a balanced life. Because of the long hours I worked, it became difficult for me to maintain some things that were going on in my personal life. As a result, I lost personal relationships and sometimes didn't take as good care of myself as I had planned. But remember, you must always find ways to do that.

It is your responsibility, not the responsibility of your institution, to make sure that you maintain all things outside of your job. In this chapter, I share tips that will help you to better balance your work and home life.

Tip #1: Have friends and friendships that are not all work-related.

One of the biggest problems as a student affairs professional is that, because you spend so much time at your work, the duality between work and personal life sometimes gets blended. As a result, many of your friends who are in a profession or work at your job also become your personal friends.

While there is nothing wrong in this, you also want friendships that are not work-related. This diversity gives you an opportunity to step away from your job every now and then. So have relationships that are not all work-related. It keeps you from being consumed with only one aspect of your life.

Tip #2: Put a system in place and try to hold to this system.

Here, a system means making sure that you do things on a weekly basis that will help your mind and body. For example, when I was working in Residence Life, I made sure that every other day, or three times a week, I went to the gym.

Your system becomes a routine, like, "I want to make sure that I go to bed," or making sure that you drink X amount of water daily, or that you spend time with your spouse or significant other every Friday night or once a week. Put systems in place that you can commit to and that give you some level of normalcy.

Tip # 3: Make sure that your family and friends are always on board and support you in what you do.

This profession is very time-consuming and often can consume much of your time and energy. As a result, you can become disengaged in your relationships with family members very easily. If you are married, be sure to confirm with your spouse that this is where you want to go. If you are not spending time with the important people in your relationships, then you might lose them, and no job is worth that.

Tip #4: This is a station in life, not your life.

Most of us are passionate about our jobs and all that we do, but for many of us, this is just where we are right now. This does not define who we are. Our success and failure in this job does not tell the complete story of where we are or who we are in our life. Remember that it is not about your station; it is about the totality of life. It is not only about where you are, but also where you want to be.

Tip #5: Name your price in the beginning.

Naming your price is very important, because if you don't name your price, you may find yourself doing things you never thought imaginable, or that you never thought you were capable of doing. It's also important as it pertains to your job and what you expect to get out of it. If the job is getting more from you than you are getting from it, or if it is not balanced in some way, then it may be time to reassess your commitment and your time.

Tip #6: Be sure to build in time for yourself.

Careers in this profession and other organizations are notorious for leaving you little to no time for yourself or for reflection. So as you strive for your professional and life goals, always build in time for yourself and reflection.

Always keep your goals in mind and how you plan to achieve those goals. Ask yourself, "How did this week go?" What do you plan to do differently going into the next week? These reflective questions will help you not only to become a better professional, but also a better person. And isn't that what it's all about?

Tip #7: When you are off, you are off.

I remember being in a relationship, and it was very difficult for me to just turn off my mind from my job. And that was one of the biggest mistakes, because no one you are with wants to hear about your job, even after you are out of your job. And while it may be very difficult, understand that it is very healthy for you to turn off from your job from time to time.

Tip #8: Watch what you eat.

An old adage says, "You are what you eat," and nothing could be closer to the truth. In our profession, many times it's very difficult to get a good, balanced meal because of work schedules. It's your responsibility to find a diet or a meal plan that works for you.

Not everything works for everybody, but make sure that your health doesn't suffer, because once your health goes, what else do you really have? Watch what you eat and have a balanced diet. It will help you to become a better professional, so you can balance out these areas.

Tip #9: Don't be a slave to the immediate.

It's very tempting to be more reactive than it is to be proactive, and in doing so we become a slave to the immediate. It's important to find ways to figure out what is a priority. What is urgent? What is an emergency? What are some things that can wait?

It may take some time if this is your first position, but usually, you can figure out a system of what works, what can wait, and what needs your attention in the very near future.

Find a way to balance priorities, because if you don't, you will always be on the never-ending hamster wheel. Keep on track, in terms of not being a slave to the immediate, and take care of things on an as-needed basis, not an immediate basis.

Things to Consider

1. What day-to-day practice do you consider as your strongest and also your weakest?

2. If you could have the perfect month, what would the ideal daily routine look like? Write down five things you can implement immediately to make this routine happen.

    a)

    b)

    c)

    d)

    e)

3. What personal and professional actions do you need to take immediately that you have been dreading, that could have the greatest impact on your results?

4. What can you do to improve how you manage your time?

CHAPTER 14

What's Next?

"When you really start doing what you love to do, you'll never work a day in your life." Brian Tracy

Use your skills to obtain your next opportunity. As an advisor or director of a program, you have been equipped with an arsenal of transferable skills that will serve you well, not just in your next position, but also for the rest of your life.

Don't shy away from or be bashful about all of the skills that you have acquired. Use them as an opportunity to sell yourself in your next situation. There are very few positions that give you opportunities to deal with crisis intervention, event planning, supervising, leadership building, team building, assessing learning outcomes, communication, and dealing with conflict

Here's the key: Don't just look at it as an opportunity to build upon your career and higher education, unless, of course, that's what you want to do. See it as opportunity to use all of the skills you acquire to understand that you can take this anywhere and do anything with it.

In this chapter, I provide tips to help you consider what your next moves might be and how to seize those opportunities.

Tip #1: Explore ALL possibilities.

Whether you decide to move on to graduate school, take another promotion, or pursue a different experience altogether, be confident that you already have the tools you need to be successful. All of the professional experiences you have been afforded will make you a better, more marketable candidate in your next position.

Use a bit of imagination and ask yourself how you can use these skills to better impact other people you may serve, as you leave this situation or this position.

Tip #2: Going to grad school.

Let's say that you decide to go to grad school. Just remember that the skills you have gained also can be used there. You still use time management and communication skills, and a number of other skills. Allow those opportunities to pay for your graduate school experience.

Tip #3: It's all a learning experience.

No matter what your experience may have been at the institution, good or bad, be encouraged and take something away with you from the experience. Many people are so disappointed after leaving the institution, because it wasn't what they thought it was going to be, and they didn't think it would end up like it did.

Regardless of your experience, you were given an opportunity to improve yourself. Sometimes disappointments are really the things we need to define who we are. Never lose sight of the fact that your disappointments or your successes at an institution are only stepping stones to your next move.

Things to Consider

1. What skill set have you acquired that will make you more marketable in another profession?

2. If you had all the money in the world, what would you do without payments?

3. What skills and areas of experience do you believe serve as your strongest assets?

4. List the pros and cons of going back to school.

   Pros: Cons:

5. List the pros and cons of acquiring a new position.

   Pros: Cons:

6. List the pros and cons of staying where you are.

   Pros: Cons:

7. Where do you see yourself in the next 2 years? The next 5 years? The next 10 years?

APPENDIX A

Program Ideas/Student Issues
By Month

FALL SEMESTER

August/September	Student Issues
Adult Literacy Awareness	Adjustment
Jazz	Roommate Conflicts
Library Card Sign-Up	Residence Halls/Room Change
National Chicken	Academics/Finances
National Piano	Emotional
National School Success	Social Rejection
Self-Improvement	Community Agreements/Service
National Cholesterol	Time Management
Education & Awareness	Homesickness
Classical Music	Campus Familiarization
International Visitors	Alcohol and Drugs
National Honey	International Student
National Courtesy	Hall Council Involvement
National Rice	Long-distance Relationships
Pleasure Your Mate	Computer Access/Usage
Women of Achievement	Policies and Procedures
National Alcohol & Drug	Values Exploration-Personal
Treatment	Beliefs
Hispanic Heritage	
911 Remembrance	
Hurricane Katrina	

FALL SEMESTER

October	Student Issues
American Magazine	Alcohol Issues
Computer Learning	Roommate Conflict-Privacy &
Crime Prevention	"Stuff"
Ending Hunger	Health & Fitness
Fire Prevention	Personal Safety
Hunger Awareness	Time Conflicts between
Lupus Awareness	Academics & Social
National AIDS Awareness	Relationships: Dating and Non-
National Car Care	dating, Student Withdrawal –
National Education	Adjustment
National Popcorn Poppin'	Friendship
Polish-American Heritage	Judicial Process
National Seafood	Advance Enrollment Planning
Hispanic Heritage	Disenchantment with School
Italian-American Heritage	Academics – Midterms
& Culture	Study Skills
Auto Battery Safety	Values Exploration – Sexuality
Consumer Information	Homesickness (Homecoming)
National Domestic	Job Panic for Mid-year Grads
Violence Awareness	Group Identity
Healthy Lung	Problems
International Book Fair	Financial Strain
Vegetarian Awareness	Involvement Opportunities
Lesbian & Gay History	Room Reassignments
Lock-in Safety	Halloween
National Breast Cancer	
National Dessert	
National Pasta	
National Pizza	
National Pork	
Value of Play	
National Disability	

FALL SEMESTER

November/Dec.	Student Issues
Good Nutrition	Finals/Grades
National Diabetes	Changing Relationships
National Epilepsy	Friends from Home
Awareness	Significant Others
World AIDS Day	Parents
National Philately	Time Management Conflicts
Religion & Philosophy	Economic Anxieties
Books	Roommate Problems – Short
Latino American	Tempers
Peanut Butter Lover's	Holiday Break Plans
Native American Heritage	Depression
International Creative	Results of Procrastination
Child & Adult	Stress
	Social Apathy
	Problems Related to Alcohol
	Health Issues

131

SPRING SEMESTER

January	Student Issues
Crime Stoppers	Academics
Soup	Post-holiday Depression
Volunteer Blood Donor	Roommate Relationships
National Eye Care	Community Agreements
Hot Tea	Revisited
Oatmeal	Involvement
Martin Luther King Jr.	Leadership
Day	Social/Academic Balance
	Family Loss/Stress
	New Environment
	New Residents
	Weight Gain
	Health Issues
	Money Problems
	Human Diversity

SPRING SEMESTER

February	Student Issues
African American History	Cabin Fever
Canned Food	Summer Job Hunting
World Understanding	Graduation Planning
Creative Romance	Cleanliness in Common Areas
National Blah-Buster	Interpersonal Communication
Humpback Whales	Living Arrangements for Fall
Awareness	Tutoring Services
International Boost Your	Race Issues
Self-Esteem	Sexuality Issues – Safe Sex
American History	Romance & Dating
American Heart	Alcohol & Relationships
National Condom	Depression
Black History	Where to Study
National Snack Food	
National Weddings	

SPRING SEMESTER

March	Student Issues
American Red Cross	Safe Spring Break
National Frozen Food	Travel Tips
National Peanut	Alcohol
Irish-American Heritage	Goal Setting – Choosing a Major
National Nutrition	Existential Crises for Seniors
National Women's History	Was My Education Worth Anything?
	Did I Choose the Wrong Major?
	Job Interview Anxiety for Seniors
	Women's Issues
	Values Clarification
	Career Services
	What Now?
	Resume Writing
	Resume Building
	Summer Job Hunting
	Money for Spring Break

SPRING SEMESTER

April	Student Issues
Keep America Beautiful	Health Issues
Listening Awareness	Sexual Assault Issues as Weather
Multicultural	Becomes Nicer
Communication	Food Service Concerns
National Recycling	Financial Strain Affects Social
National STDs Education	Life
& Awareness	Community Issues
Actors Appreciation	Noise as Weather Gets Warmer
Alcohol Awareness	Public Trash Issues
National Anxiety	Time Management
National Humor	Mating Season
National Poetry	Pressure of Selecting a Major
Stress Awareness	Illness due to Weather Changes

SPRING SEMESTER

May	Student Issues
Better Sleep	Take Back the Night
Electrical Safety	Closure for Communities
Mental Health	Closing Procedures
National Barbecue	Year is Ending
National Hamburger	Finals Pressure
National Egg	Worry about Going Home for
National High Blood	the Summer
Pressure	Health & Fitness
Asian/Pacific American	Academics
Heritage	Frustration
Revise Your Work Schedule	Disappointment
National Sasquatch	Senior Job Panic
Month of Peace	Moving
National Asparagus	Depression
National Bike	Separation Anxiety
National Mime	
National Physical Fitness	
& National Photo Sports	
National Strawberry	
Personal History	
Awareness	
Cinco de Mayo (Mexico)	
National Salad	

SPRING SEMESTER

June	Student Issues
Fresh Fruits & Vegetables	Paying for Summer School
Fireworks Safety	Transferring Credit
National Accordion	Transitioning into Career
Awareness	Gaining Meaningful Summer
National Drive Safe	Experiences
National Pest Control	
Supreme Court Month of	
Tough Decisions	
Gay Pride	
Black Music	
Tony Award	
June Dairy	
Youth Suicide Prevention	
Zoo & Aquarium	

APPENDIX B

Creative Programs on a Shoestring Budget

No matter the size of your organization, here is a list of programs that you can implement regardless of your budget:

- ☑ Ask a business professor or money management guru to give a lecture on personal finances.
- ☑ Host a potluck dinner with professors.
- ☑ Host an old school Saturday morning cartoons breakfast.
- ☑ Co-sponsor a résumé writing clinic with the office of Career Services.
- ☑ Co-sponsor a mock interview clinic with the office of Career Services.
- ☑ Host a workshop on how to build and improve your credit score conducted with a finance expert.

- ☑ Hold a graduate student meet and greet forum where students relate what they wish they had known earlier about graduate school.
- ☑ Rent the gym and do a basketball or other type of sports tournament.
- ☑ Collect canned goods for the less fortunate and donate them to a food drop.
- ☑ Have a residential hall decoration contest.
- ☑ Have a building decoration contest in conjunction with homecoming.
- ☑ Hold an ice cream social.
- ☑ Host a study break; serve coffee and cake.
- ☑ Host a healthy study break; serve healthy foods and offer nutrition lists.
- ☑ Ask a physical education/health faculty member to talk about weight training, training for a marathon, or healthy eating.
- ☑ Host a cooking contest like "Top Chef" or chili cooking contest or a desert sampling.
- ☑ Do an artist cover, like Lady Gaga, Michael Jackson, or another popular artist.
- ☑ Hold a fashion show with or without a twist.

- ☑ Replicate a popular TV show like "American Idol" or "The Voice."
- ☑ Hold relationship forums where men and women talk about relationship issues.
- ☑ Sponsor a series of computer learning clinics where people can learn basic and advanced software skills.
- ☑ Host a field day.
- ☑ Host an arts & crafts night.
- ☑ Host a karaoke night.
- ☑ Hold a discussion forum about a controversial movie, book, topic, or other current events hosted by a professor or fan of that topic.
- ☑ Host a lock-in, out-all-night event where students participate in activities overnight.
- ☑ Hold a marathon dance competition.
- ☑ Host a 10K run on campus.
- ☑ Provide community service at a local shelter or a church.
- ☑ Provide alternative programming on Friday and Saturday nights.

- ☑ Sponsor a particular team on a sports night and wear team colors, or have a funny hat night at sports home games.
- ☑ On Halloween night or Christmas invite the local community to your campus and have faculty/staff members dress for the occasion.
- ☑ Hire a diversity lecturer.
- ☑ Hire a leadership expert.
- ☑ Host a passport drive where people can apply for a passport.
- ☑ Host an international fair, festival, and/or parade.
- ☑ Host a video game tournament.

These are just some ideas for a shoestring budget that could be implemented and work well on most campuses. Use your creativity and that of your organization to add to this list.

APPENDIX C
Sample Activity Calendars
Fall Semester

Event		Competency Addressed	Month
New Student Leader Training		Leadership	August
Back to School Rally		College Completion	August
Personal Finance 101		Life Skills	August
Student Organizational Fair		Leadership	September
Video Game Tournament		Social	September
Hispanic Heritage Month Events		Diversity	September/October
The Campus Resource Scavenger Hunt		College Completion	September
Midnight Breakfast		Social	September
Leadership Retreat for Clubs		Leadership	October
Sport Team Appreciation Week		Social	October
Midterm Study Break		Academic Support	October
Sophomore Support Week		Academic Support	October
International Week		Diversity	November
Chili Cook-off/Food Drive		Social Community Service	November
Stress Free Comedy Show		Social	December
World AIDS Event		Social Justice	December
Clothes Drive		Community Service	December
Final Study Break		Academic	December

Sample Activity Calendar
Spring Semester

Event	Competency Addressed	Month
Mid-Year Leadership Retreat	Leadership	January
New Student Orientation	College Completion	January
Martin Luther King Day	Diversity	January
Black History Month Events	Diversity	February
Themed Fashion/Talent Show	Social	Feb/March
Resume Writing/Interview Skills	Life Skills	February
Video Game Tournament	Social	February
Mardi Gras Celebration	Diversity	Feb/March
Aspiring Club Officer Q & A	Leadership	Feb/March
Student Elections/Training	Leadership	Feb/March
Midterm Study Break	Academic Support	March
Spring Break Activities	Social/Service Learning	March
Take Back the Night	Social Justice	March/April
Spades/Poker Tournament	Social	March
Into the Real World Week	Life Skills	March/April
Women's History Month Events	Diversity	March
Appreciation Awards Ceremony	Social	April
Final Study Break	Academic Support	April/May
Charity Drive	Community Service	April/May

APPENDIX D
Sample Forms/Promotional Materials

Sample Meeting Format:

1. Sign In
2. Ice Breaker: New Member/First Time Attendees Acknowledgement
3. New Business/Discussion/Vote
4. Old Business/Discussion/Vote
5. Committee Reports
6. Closing Announcements
7. End

Additional Tips:

* Appoint a weekly note keeper.
* Always try to leave the meeting on a positive note.
* Appoint a weekly timekeeper.
* Remember, it's about the quality of things you get accomplished. It's not about how long your meetings are.

Tips for Student Leaders and Advisors in Creating a Good Activity:

1. **Think of cost.**

   Come up with inexpensive but enjoyable activities. *Up Your Org: A Guide to Help Student Leaders Thrive* offers a variety of events, activities and programs that are very cost-effective and fun.

2. **Location.**

   Getting to an activity or event is also a concern, so try to plan activities and/or events around or near campus to save on gas and transportation costs. This also cuts down on concerns about how to get to an event or activity.

3. **Time of day.**

   This will be a major obstacle for everyone. At least one person will always have a conflict with what you are planning. However, there are obvious times to avoid planning something. For example, days before a test are not a good time to plan things, unless it is a planned study session.

4. **Try to plan activities of interest to all backgrounds.**

   Think of the cultural topics that will be discussed throughout the year. Talk to some of your members and friends to see if they have any suggestions. Remember that the activities are not about your interests, but in connecting the students to you and your school. The activities are merely a vehicle for doing that.

5. **Suggestions.**

   ✓ Plan an activity just before or after lunch, or whenever you notice students hanging out.
   ✓ Plan a study session before a test with tutors.
   ✓ Survey your students, ask them what they want.
   ✓ Go to a sporting event.

Event Planning: Who, What, When, Where, Why, and How

Who are you planning this meeting for? Who is your target or intended audience?

What do you want to do? Describe the activity and what would be a successful outcome as a result of the event.

When will the event take place? Is there a timeline/deadline?

Where will the event take place?

Why do you want to do this event? Is this event a need or a want? For whom?

How do you plan to execute the event? Who is doing what? How much money will the event cost? How will you promote the event? How will you evaluate the event? How will you know if it is a success?

Sample Evaluation Form

Overall Evaluation of Event

Your Name:
Name of Event/Program:

We would really like for you to attend another sponsored event in the future. What's the best way to contact you?

Email: Twitter:
Facebook: Phone:

Please take a moment to answer the following questions. Your comments are an important contribution as we design events to meet your needs.

How did you hear about this event?

What will you do differently in your life as a result of this event?

How can we improve this program/event?

What other kinds of activities/events would you like to attend?

Please rate the following statements using a 1 through 5 scale:

_____ I can immediately apply the information in my life.
_____ The presentation met my educational needs.
_____ As a result of this event, I feel more connected to this community.

Event Marking **Email #1**
(To Be Sent <u>Two Weeks BEFORE</u> the event)

Dear _____ :

Hello. I hope this email finds you well. On (INSERT DATE/TIME/PLACE HERE), we will be hosting _____. This event will reinforce many of the institution's values, and we hope both you and your students will participate in this extraordinary event.

We are very excited to be hosting _____. We believe that your students will get a great deal out of this event because _____.

Please take a moment to review the following information _____, which provides all the information you need about this event. **See attachment.**

We ask that you consider making the event mandatory for all your students. If this option is not possible, we ask that you at least consider offering extra credit for the students who attend.

If I can be of assistance in any way, please do not hesitate to let me know.

Thank you for helping us make a difference in the lives of our students.

Name: *Title:*

Phone Number: *E-Mail:*

Event Marketing <u>Email #2</u>
(To be sent <u>One Week BEFORE</u> the event)

Dear _____:

Just a reminder that _____ will be happening on our campus on (INSERT DAY/TIME/PLACE HERE).

If you haven't already done so, please announce this presentation to your students and encourage them to attend.

We also ask that you consider making the event mandatory or offering extra credit for those who attend.

Remember this _____ may be one of the few (and for some the *only*) time they can hear completely unbiased information they can use to improve their academic and social well-being.

Thank you in advance for your support. If I can be of any assistance, please do not hesitate to contact me.

Name: *Title:*

Phone Number: *E-Mail:*

150

Event Marketing Final Email
(To be sent the <u>Day BEFORE</u> the event)

Dear _____ :

Just a final reminder that our _____ will be tomorrow. The event will take place on our campus at (INSERT DAY/TIME/PLACE HERE).

If you haven't done so already, please announce the event to your students and encourage them to attend. If possible, we ask that you consider making the event a requirement for all your students or at the very least offering extra credit to those who attend.

Thank you in advance for your support. If I can be of assistance in any way, please do not hesitate to contact me.

Name: *Title:*

Phone Number: *E-Mail:*

Professional Organizations List

National Association of Campus Activities

www.NACA.org

Association for the Promotion of Campus Activities

www.APCA.com

Association of Fraternity Advisors

www.FraternityAdvisors.org

National Orientation Directors Association

www.NODAweb.org

National Association of Colleges & Employers

www.NACEweb.org

National Conference of Student Services

www.MagnaPubs.com

Student Leadership Conferences

www.StudentLeader.com

National Panhellenic Conference

www.SEPCOnline.net

National Society of Collegiate Scholars

www.NSCS.org

National African American Student Leadership
Conference

www.NAASLC.org

International Honor Society of Two-Year Colleges

www.PTK.org

North American Association of Commencement Officers

www.naaco.info

Association of College Unions International

www.ACUI.org

Southern Association for College Student Affairs

www.sacsa.org

National Career Development Association

http://ncda.org

American Association of Community Colleges

www.aacc.nche.edu

American Association of University Women

www.AAUW.org

Jesuit Association of Student Personnel Administrators

http://jaspa.creighton.edu

Student Affairs Professionals

www.StudentAffairs.org

Golden Key International Honor Society

www.GoldenKey.org

American Student Association of Community Colleges

www.ASACC.org

Recommended Reading

Head, Heart and Guts: How the World's Best Companies Develop Complete Leaders, by David L. Dotlich

The One Minute Manager, by Ken Blanchard

Leading Change, by John P. Kotter

The Time Trap: The Classic Book on Time Management, by R. Alec Mackenzie

How to Delegate (Essential Managers Series), by Robert Heller

The Manager's Guide to Effective Meetings, by Barbara J. Streibel

Getting Things Done: The Art of Stress-Free Productivity, by David Allen

The 7 Habits of Highly Effective People, by Stephen R. Covey

Up Your ORG: A Guide to Help Student Leaders Thrive, by Tawan Perry

Get Everyone in Your Boat Rowing in the Same Direction: 5 Leadership Principles to Follow So Others Will Follow You, by Bob Boylan

Recommended Reading for Team Building Activities

Quick Team-Building Activities for Busy Managers: 50 Exercises That Get Results in Just 15 Minutes, by Brian Cole Miller

1001 Ways to Reward Employees, by Bob Nelson, Ph.D.

365 Low or No Cost Workplace Teambuilding Activities: Games and Exercises Designed to Build Trust & Encourage Teamwork Among Employees, by John N. Peragine

101 Teambuilding Activities: Ideas Every Coach Can Use to Enhance Teamwork, Communication and Trust, by Greg Dale and Scott Conant

ABOUT THE AUTHOR

 Tawan Perry, M.Ed., is a student leadership expert and an award winning author. As an undergraduate student, he served as both SGA Vice President and as a resident assistant. After graduating from college, he worked at various institutions as a housing administrator, Greek advisor, and assistant dean.

Today, Tawan is a nationally renowned student leadership expert who has been featured in various magazines, talk shows, and printed media. He currently resides in Raleigh, N.C. For more information visit www.tawanperry.com

More Products from Tawan Perry

College Sense: What College and High School Advisors Don't Tell You about College

Making sense of higher education can confound the most stellar of students. Your college education isn't just about gaining knowledge, but an experience unlike any other you will have in life. Navigating the college environment is about learning the language: If you know how the system works, you can understand and prepare for the complexities that college presents.

It explores a myriad of essential topics such as how to reduce and eliminate debt, the questions that you should ask during your campus visit, and how to get the most of your college experience. It's the only book you'll ever need to help you prepare for all those things that your advisors didn't tell you about college. *College Sense* **was the 2008 National Best Books award winner for college guides.**

College Sense is ideal for:

☑ Any incoming first year student

☑ High school or PTA that want to give graduating seniors an invaluable gift

☑ Any community college student that will be transferring into a 4-year institution

☑ Non-profit organizations that want to give students an advantage in college

☑ University 101 college course textbook

College Sense for Parents

Each year college becomes gradually more expensive, and families find themselves desperately looking for ways to reduce rising costs. *College Sense for Parents* offers help by providing several time-tested strategies that will eliminate debt and reduce the cost of college. This audio recording covers topics such as how to reduce the cost of tuition, board, books, application fees, and other related college expenses. Listen to it on your way to work or in the comfort of your home. *College Sense for Parents* gets straight to the point and offers tips that will easily save you thousands of dollars. This is a **must have** for any parent with college bound children.

Quote These (College Edition)

Whether you are an incoming freshmen or a procrastinating senior, ***Quote These*** is the most astounding book of quotes ever assembled to assist and inspire college students. Categorized by such themes as transition, relationships and time management, this book is a great resource whether you're writing speeches, personal statements, essays, or just looking for guidance during those often riddle filled college years.

Students Go to College For Free: How to Get a B.S. without the B.S.

If you're stressed out about how to pay for your college education or looking for a way to get your degree without going into a lifetime of debt, *Students Go to College For Free* has the solution. A **must read** book for students at all levels, advisors and counselors too, this book shows you how to attend a tuition-free college, attend prestigious schools without the ACT or SAT, get your master's degree and doctorate for free, pay in-state tuition even if you're out of state, and how to earn 30 or more college credits before taking a college class.

Up Your Org: A Guide to Help Student Leaders Thrive

A GUIDE TO HELP
STUDENT LEADERS THRIVE
TAWAN PERRY

This hands-on guide is a blueprint of how to be a successful campus leader, packed with information and tools to equip you to become a great student leader, whatever your position is in the organization. Student leaders will discover: how to run more efficient and fun meetings that still get things done; how to get buy-in, even from apathetic students; effective ways to partner well with administration and other campus organizations; new ways to create a more inclusive and safer campus community; how to create dynamic programs that will be well attended even on a shoestring budget, and ways to re-energize your student organization in the best and worst of times.

Editor

Cynthia Bull is an internationally published writer and editor who helps international authors, marketers and speakers add greater value to their products through her top-quality writing, editing and transcription services. She is the author of *How To Be A Medical Transcriptionist* and *Winning At Work While Balancing Your Life,* a contributing author of *Walking with the Wise Entrepreneur* (Mentors Publishing House), cited in *Make BIG Profits on eBay* (Entrepreneur Press), and Managing Editor of *Mentors Magazine Think & Grow Rich Edition.*

Cynthia has created over 400 book products in recent years for her clients and is a contributing writer for an online organization dedicated to helping small businesses succeed. As mentor, Cynthia helps clients reach their goals through her products, experience, and genuine caring. For more information she can be contacted at:

www.cynrje.com
www.cynrjetranscription.com

29955477R00094

Made in the USA
Charleston, SC
30 May 2014